PLANT-EATING DINOSAURS

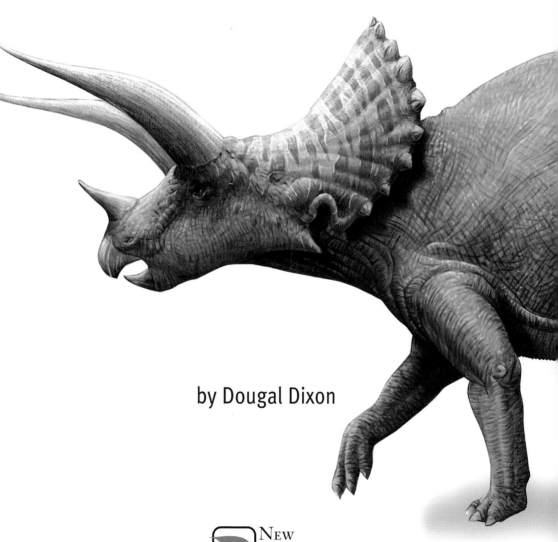

by Dougal Dixon

NEW
FOREST
PRESS

CONTENTS

Publisher: Tim Cook
Editor: Guy Croton
Designer: Carol Davis
Production Controller: Ed Green
Production Manager: Suzy Kelly

ISBN: 978-1-84898-333-5
Library of Congress Control Number: 2010925201
Tracking number: nfp0006

North American edition copyright
© TickTock Entertainment Ltd. 2010
First published in North America in 2010 by
New Forest Press, PO Box 784, Mankato, MN 56002
www.newforestpress.com

Printed in the USA
9 8 7 6 5 4 3 2 1

PLANT-EATING DINOSAURS

INTRODUCTION

The biggest land animals of all time, that's what they were! The great plant-eating dinosaurs of Jurassic and Cretaceous periods. Far larger than the biggest of the meat-eaters. Nowadays we have elephants and rhinoceroses, but nothing on the scale of these great creatures of the Mesozoic Era.

The sauropods were the biggest of them—huge bodies with little heads mounted on incredibly long necks and whip-like tails. Even the smallest of these—dwarf forms that lived on islands—were bigger than most animals that we have nowadays. These great behemoths were close relatives, believe it or not, of the smaller meat-eating dinosaurs.

Then we have the ornithopods. These were quite different and started off as small two-footed plant-eating dinosaurs. They mostly stayed in the shadows of the mighty sauropods for the first half of the age of dinosaurs, but then, with the dawning of the Cretaceous period, they came into their own. From sprinting rat-sized animals they evolved into big beasts, as big as trucks, that were the most important of the plant-eaters across North America and the rest of the northern continents. These "duckbills," big though they were, never reached the great sizes of the sauropods.

Related to the ornithopods were the various types of armored dinosaurs.

Stegosaurids came first. With plates on their backs and spikes on their tails, they could defend themselves against the meat-eaters of the Jurassic. In some forms the armored plates became adapted for other purposes such as display and perhaps temperature regulation. In any case these became the most flamboyant dinosaurs of the time—the peacocks of the Jurassic period.

Come the Cretaceous the stegosaurids began to die away and were replaced by the tank-like ankylosaurids and nodosaurids. These were protected by an armor of bony studs covered in horn, that ran from the head, down the neck, and back and right down the tail in a continuous pavement. They also carried defensive weapons—shoulder spikes in the case of the nodosaurids and tail clubs in the ankylosaurids.

Late arrivals on the dinosaur scene were the ceratopsians—the horned dinosaurs. These evolved from the smaller two-footed ornithopods. Their jaws became more powerful in response to a change of diet to tougher plants, and their skulls sported heavy bony ridges to anchor the strong mouth muscles. These bony ridges

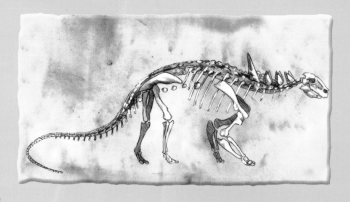

then evolved into big armor and display structures. The heavier heads obliged the animals to abandon their two-footed existence and go about on all fours, and finally defensive horns developed on the massive skulls.

As is normal in the natural world, all these evolutionary developments came about because of changes in the environment, especially in the vegetation. As new types of plants evolved, then new types of animal with different food-gathering techniques and different jaw structures, evolved to take advantage of them. Ferns gave way to flowering plants in the undergrowth, coniferous trees gave way to broadleaved trees in the forests, and all these changes were accompanied by changes in the dinosaur types. This process did not stop when the dinosaurs did. After they became extinct and the mammals took over, the continuing changes of the flora produced changes in the animal life. With the spreading of grasslands about 50 million years ago, the long-legged running grass-eating animals like horses and antelope evolved.

Look at the great mounted dinosaur skeletons in the American Museum of Natural History in New York, the Field Museum in Chicago, the Carnegie Museum of Natural History in Pittsburgh, and marvel at these wonderful animals that roamed the continents in the past. Put yourself in the position of the pioneers who first found their bones in the dry badlands of the mid-west, of the paleontologists who came to dig them up and to study them, of the industrialists and philanthropists who put up the money to sponsor their recovery and display, and of the museum directors who established the fabulous displays that allow us all to appreciate them and give us a taste of the wonderful dinosaur life of the past.

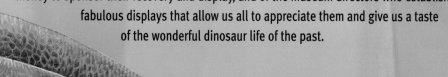

THE FIRST PLANT-EATING DINOSAURS

Plant-eating dinosaurs (herbivores) were the real giants of the Mesozoic Era. Among their ranks were the mighty *Diplodocus* and *Brachiosaurus*, the largest animals ever to walk our planet. Herbivorous reptiles are known from the early part of the Carboniferous Period, 350 million years ago. The first herbivorous dinosaurs evolved in the Late Triassic Period, appearing about the same time as carnivores. Because both groups of dinosaurs have similarly formed hipbones, we know that the plant eaters are closely related to meat-eating dinosaurs.

PLATEOSAURUS

The first plant-eating dinosaurs belonged to the prosauropod group. *Plateosaurus* was a typical prosauropod. It had a long neck and small head, but perhaps its most important feature was its big body. To process plant matter, a herbivore needs a far greater digestive system than a carnivore. The prosauropod's heavy mass of intestines, carried well forward of the hips, would have made the animal too unbalanced to spend much time on its hind legs, so prosauropods became four-footers early in their history.

PANGAEA

The world was very different in Late Triassic/Early Jurassic times. All the continental landmasses were together in one area, called Pangaea. This meant that animals of the same kind could migrate everywhere and is why we find the remains of almost identical animals all over the world, from Australia to North America.

TRIASSIC 248-206 MYA	EARLY/MID JURASSIC 206-159 MYA	LATE JURASSIC 159-144 MYA	EARLY CRETACEOUS 144-97 MYA	LATE CRETACEOUS 97-65 MYA

MUSSAURUS

The smallest dinosaur skeleton known belongs to a prosauropod. This *Mussaurus* is small enough to be held in the the palm of a human hand. We know it is the skeleton of a baby or an embryo, however, because the eyes and feet are bigger in relation to its body size than they would be in an adult, and its bones are not totally fused together. An adult *Mussaurus* would have been about 10 feet (3 meters) long.

SKULL COMPARISON BETWEEN A HERBIVORE AND CARNIVORE

PLATEOSAURUS

- Jaw articulates below level of teeth.
- Leaf-shaped teeth with continuous cutting edge.
- Coarsely serrated teeth for shredding leaves and shoots.
- Teeth more or less the same size.
- No gaps between teeth.

TYRANNOSAURUS

- Jaw articulates at point level with teeth.
- Strong, spike-shaped, piercing teeth used for gripping and killing.
- Finely serrated saw-edged teeth like a steak knife.
- Teeth often break off and new ones grow in their place, creating a snaggle-toothed appearance.
- Teeth have gaps between them.

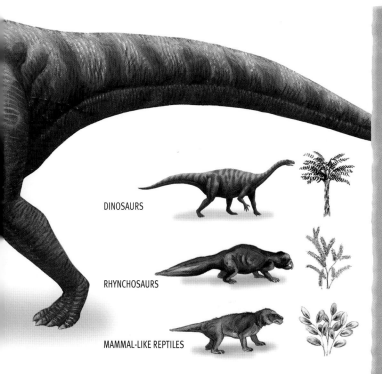

DINOSAURS

RHYNCHOSAURS

MAMMAL-LIKE REPTILES

DEVELOPING VEGETATION

In the early part of the age of reptiles, the most prolific plant, a fern with seeds, was the primary food source of the main plant-eating animals, the mammal-like reptiles. The seed ferns died away during the Triassic Period, and ferns more like our modern species became common. Another group, the rhynchosaurs, evolved to eat them. At the end of the Triassic, conifer trees spread everywhere, and prosauropod dinosaurs evolved to eat them.

LIFE OF THE PROSAUROPODS

E ver since plants have existed, plant-eating animals have fed on them, and ever since plant-eating animals have existed, meat eaters have, in turn, fed on them. This type of food chain can still be seen on the grasslands of Africa, where herds of herbivorous wildebeest and zebra graze on low vegetation and are preyed on by prowling carnivores such as lions and cheetahs. It was no different with dinosaurs. Prosauropods fed on the trees and were themselves stalked by meat eaters.

TRACKWAYS

The footprints called *Navajopus* from Lower Jurassic rocks of Arizona perfectly match the foot bones of a typical prosauropod, with big hind feet and smaller front feet, each with four toes and inwardly curved claws. They are likely to have been made by a small *Thecodontosaurus*-sized prosauropod called *Ammosaurus*.

MELANOROSAURUS

HELPLESS PREY

Paleontologists have found the remains of a prosauropod *Euskelosaurus* in Upper Triassic rocks in South Africa and Switzerland. The bones of its feet and legs are preserved, but the rest of the skeleton is broken up and scattered. Teeth of crocodile-like reptiles and carnivorous dinosaurs are among them. From this we suppose that *Euskelosaurus* became stuck in mud and, while struggling helplessly, was attacked by meat eaters.

RANGE OF PROSAUROPODS

During the Triassic and early Jurassic periods, prosauropods ranged all over Pangaea, the world's landmass. *Melanorosaurus* lived in South Africa, *Thecodontosaurus* in western Europe, *Anchisaurus* in western North America, and *Riojasaurus* in South America. Other prosauropods, such as *Plateosaurus* and the *Plateosaurus*-like *Lufengosaurus*, lived in what is now China. They were all extinct by Middle Jurassic times.

RIOJASAURUS

THECODONTOSAURUS

ANCHISAURUS

TRIASSIC	EARLY/MID JURASSIC	LATE JURASSIC	EARLY CRETACEOUS	LATE CRETACEOUS
248-206 MYA	206-159 MYA	159-144 MYA	144-97 MYA	97-65 MYA

SAUROPODS

The biggest dinosaurs were long-necked plant eaters known as sauropods ("lizard feet"). They had elephantine bodies, legs like tree trunks, small heads on top of long necks, and long, whiplike tails. They were related to the meat-eating dinosaurs and to the prosauropods, evolving in the Early Jurassic and dying off in Cretaceous times.

TRACES OF LIFESTYLE

We used to think sauropods were too heavy to spend much time on land and must have supported their vast bulk by wading in deep water. However, we now know (mostly from fossilized footprints) that sauropods moved about in herds on dry land. Large and small footprints found together show that different sauropods lived in groups. Because there is no sign of tail marks in the tracks, they must have kept their tails raised.

DIPLODOCUS

Perhaps the best known of the long sauropods is *Diplodocus*. At 88 feet (27 m) long, it was one of several sauropods that roamed North America in Late Jurassic times. The way the neck bones were articulated tells us they browsed on low ferny vegetation, probably sweeping out great arcs with their long necks.

TRIASSIC 248-206 MYA	EARLY/MID JURASSIC 206-159 MYA	LATE JURASSIC 159-144 MYA	EARLY CRETACEOUS 144-97 MYA	LATE CRETACEOUS 97-65 MYA

SAUROPOD FRAME

Remains of sauropod skeletons consist of massive pieces of fossilized bone, so big there is nothing alive today that compares with them. In one of the latest techniques, pioneered by Prof. Kent Stephens of the University of Oregon, very basic bone shapes are programed into a computer and manipulated to let us see how the various pieces moved against one another.

STOMACH STONES

The small head and mouth of sauropods were not designed for chewing. To help break down food, they swallowed stones, which ground up plant material. We know this because gastroliths (stomach stones) have been found among their bones. Today, many plant-eating birds do the same.

SHUNOSAURUS

DIPLODOCUS

IN DEFENSE

Sauropods would have been prey to the big carnivorous dinosaurs. Just as today tigers do not attack fully grown elephants, in Jurassic times the biggest of the sauropods would have been safe from the meat eaters, but the young and the sick would have been under constant threat. *Diplodocus* probably protected itself and its herd by using its long tapering tail as a whip. *Shunosaurus*, which lived in China during the Middle Jurassic, probably used the small club on the end of its tail to defend itself.

THE HEYDAY OF THE SAUROPODS

During the Late Jurassic, sauropods were at their most widespread. Some were long and low and browsed low vegetation. Others were tall and browsed lower branches of trees. There were two main types, as distinguished by the shape of their teeth. *Diplodocus* and the other long, low sauropods had peglike teeth, while the taller, stouter sauropods, such as *Brachiosaurus*, had thick, spoon-shaped teeth that indicate a different type of feeding arrangement. However, nobody is sure what it was.

DINOSAUR DETECTIVES

Often, when the remains of a very big animal are discovered, there are tantalizingly few bones found. Comparing them directly to a more complete skeleton can give us some idea of the kind of animal they came from. In 1999, four neck vertebrae of a gigantic sauropod were found. The *Sauroposeidon* bones turned out to be very similar to the neck bones of *Brachiosaurus*. So we are fairly sure *Sauroposeidon* was an animal very much like *Brachiosaurus*—but bigger!

SEISMOSAURUS

The longest dinosaur known used to be called *Seismosaurus*, like *Diplodocus* but much bigger. The only remains so far found suggested an animal that was about 164 feet (50 meters) long when it was alive. However more recent studies make it much shorter—about 115 feet (35 meters), and show that it was actually a species of *Diplodocus*. It is now called *Diplodocus hallorum* (the best known species is *D. carnegii*).

BRACHIOSAURUS

Although many remains have been found in the Morrison Formation, the best skeleton of *Brachiosaurus* was found halfway across the globe in Tanzania. This shows that in Late Jurassic times, Pangaea (*see page 6*) had not yet split completely and the same types of dinosaur lived all over the world. A German expedition unearthed this skeleton in 1909, when Tanzania was known as German East Africa. The complete skeleton, the biggest mounted anywhere, is in the Humboldt Museum in Berlin. Recently it has been found that this skeleton is different enough from the American specimens to earn it its own name. It is now called *Giraffatitan*.

APATOSAURUS GROWTH RATE

It is difficult to tell how long a dinosaur lived. Sometimes, growth lines in the bones (like the rings of trees) suggest the animal grew more quickly at some time each year. Its age can be assessed by counting the lines. Studies of the bones of *Apatosaurus* (previously known as *Brontosaurus*), a relative of *Diplodocus*, suggest these sauropods grew quickly, without growth rings, for about 10 years. By then, they had reached 90 percent of their adult size.

10 YEARS

TRIASSIC	EARLY/MID JURASSIC	LATE JURASSIC	EARLY CRETACEOUS	LATE CRETACEOUS
248-206 MYA	206-159 MYA	159-144 MYA	144-97 MYA	97-65 MYA

THE LAST OF THE SAUROPODS

As the world passed from the Jurassic into the Cretaceous Period, vegetation began to change and the continents moved apart. Different dinosaurs were becoming prominent. The sauropods began to die away as a completely different group of plant-eating dinosaurs evolved. In some places, the sauropods still thrived, either because the old style vegetation still flourished in some environments or because they lived on isolated continents where the new dinosaurs did not reach. Despite the spread of the new dinosaur types, there were sauropods existing to the very end of the Mesozoic Era.

SALTASAURUS

Of the sauropods that survived into the Cretaceous Period, the titanosaurids (such as *Saltasaurus* in Argentina or *Ampelosaurus* in France) were perhaps the most successful. Despite their name, at about 39 feet (12 m) long, they were not particularly big for sauropods. In Cretaceous times there were many islands in the shallow seas. Some dwarf types of titanosaurids, no bigger than cows, evolved to live on the scant resources found there.

TOUGH GUY

The bony armor pieces from the back of a titanosaurid were found as long ago as 1890 in Madagascar. The paleontologist who first identified them was not believed, because no other sauropod was known to be covered with armor. Only with the discovery of armored titanosaurids in Argentina in the 1970s and a more complete armored titanosaurid in Madagascar in the 1990s was this scientist's theory proven correct.

DRESSED TO IMPRESS

Not only did late sauropods have armor, but some had spines and frills as well. *Amargasaurus* from Early Cretaceous Argentina had a double row of spines down its neck and a tall fin down its back. Unusual sauropods evolved in Cretaceous South America because it was an island continent, and evolution took an independent direction.

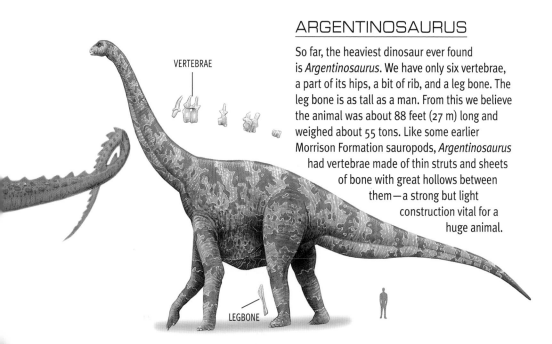

VERTEBRAE

LEGBONE

ARGENTINOSAURUS

So far, the heaviest dinosaur ever found is *Argentinosaurus*. We have only six vertebrae, a part of its hips, a bit of rib, and a leg bone. The leg bone is as tall as a man. From this we believe the animal was about 88 feet (27 m) long and weighed about 55 tons. Like some earlier Morrison Formation sauropods, *Argentinosaurus* had vertebrae made of thin struts and sheets of bone with great hollows between them—a strong but light construction vital for a huge animal.

TRIASSIC 248-206 MYA	EARLY/MID JURASSIC 206-159 MYA	LATE JURASSIC 159-144 MYA	EARLY CRETACEOUS 144-97 MYA	LATE CRETACEOUS 97-65 MYA

ORNITHOPODS
THE BIRD FEET

During the Triassic, at about the same time as meat eaters and prosauropods appeared, another group of plant eaters also originated. What made them different was their hipbones, which gave more space to the big intestines plant eaters needed yet enabled them to balance on their hind legs. Scientists in the 1800s called these plant eaters sauropods ("lizard feet") because they had a lizard-like arrangement of bones in their feet; the two-footed, bird-hipped dinosaurs they called ornithopods ("bird feet").

THREE KINDS OF TEETH

In 1976, the complete skeleton of a primitive early ornithopod *Heterodontosaurus* was discovered in South Africa. Strangely, it had three different types of teeth: sharp cutting teeth at the front, a pair of doglike fangs in both upper and lower jaw, and broad, grinding teeth. No other ornithopod had such teeth. It is almost as if evolution were trying out new designs early in the development of the group before natural selection determined the best pattern.

TRIASSIC	EARLY/MID JURASSIC	LATE JURASSIC	EARLY CRETACEOUS	LATE CRETACEOUS
248-206 MYA	206-159 MYA	159-144 MYA	144-97 MYA	97-65 MYA

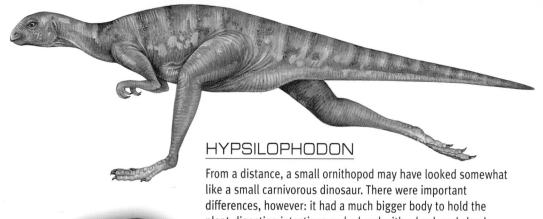

HYPSILOPHODON

From a distance, a small ornithopod may have looked somewhat like a small carnivorous dinosaur. There were important differences, however: it had a much bigger body to hold the plant-digesting intestines and a head with a beak and cheek pouches. The arms were also different, having four or five fingers rather than two or three, like meat eaters. The markings were also probably different, far more subdued than those on carnivorous dinosaurs.

HYPSILOPHODON SKULL

The skull of an ornithopod was different from that of a sauropod. There was always a beak at the front for cropping food. The teeth were not merely for raking in leaves but were designed for chewing them, either by chopping or grinding. Depressions at each side of the skull show where there were probably cheek pouches used to hold the food while it was being processed. This is a far more complicated arrangement than that of the prosauropods and sauropods.

ADVANCED JAWS

Later, more advanced ornithopods had complex chewing mechanisms. An animal like *Iguanodon (see page 18)* or a hadrosaur *(see pages 20–21)* had its upper teeth mounted on articulated plates at each side of the skull. As the lower jaw rose, these plates moved outward to allow the sloping chewing surfaces of both sets of teeth to grind past one another. This constant milling action wore away the teeth, and new ones grew to replace them.

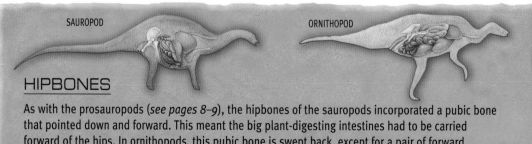

SAUROPOD ORNITHOPOD

HIPBONES

As with the prosauropods (*see pages 8–9*), the hipbones of the sauropods incorporated a pubic bone that pointed down and forward. This meant the big plant-digesting intestines had to be carried forward of the hips. In ornithopods, this pubic bone is swept back, except for a pair of forward extensions that splayed out to the side. The big plant-digesting intestines could be carried beneath the animal's hipbone, closer to its center of gravity. This enabled the ornithopod to walk on its hind legs, balanced by its tail—just like a meat-eating dinosaur.

THE IGUANODON DYNASTY

Iguanodon was among the first dinosaurs to be discovered. The teeth and a few scraps of bone were found first and were obviously from a large plant-eating reptile. At the time, few people were familiar with modern plant-eating reptiles, so the animal was particularly unusual. Some scientific work was being done on the modern South American plant-eating lizard, the iguana, which had teeth somewhat like those of this new fossil. Hence, it was given the name *Iguanodon*.

IGUANODON FOOD

Iguanodon lived in northern Europe during Early Cretaceous times. It wandered in herds across swampy landscapes, knee-deep in reed-beds of horsetail plants that grew just like our modern species. The herds probably grazed on these horsetails as they moved from one area to another.

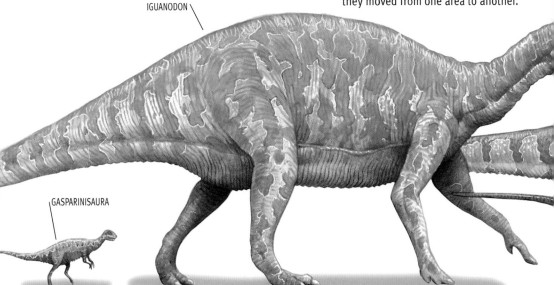

IGUANODON

GASPARINISAURA

MEET THE FAMILY

The modern view of *Iguanodon* is that it was too heavy to spend much time on its hind legs, so it moved on all fours. Since it was discovered, scientists have found many more iguanodontids. Australian *Muttaburrasaurus* was slightly smaller. American *Tenontosaurus* had a particularly long tail. The most primitive member of the group was *Gasparinisaura* from Argentina, the size of a turkey.

THE OURANOSAURUS QUESTION

One iguanodontid, *Ouranosaurus*, had an arrangement of tall spines forming a kind of picket fence along its backbone, probably to support some sort of fin or sail. Since *Ouranosaurus* lived in North Africa, which was hot and arid during Cretaceous times, such a sail could have regulated its body temperature by exposing blood vessels to the warming sun and cooling wind. A meat eater, *Spinosaurus*, lived in the same time and place and also had a sail. Another theory is that the spines supported a fatty hump, such as camels have today.

IGUANA TOOTH

The first remains of *Iguanodon*—teeth and parts of bones—were discovered in Kent in about 1822 by English country doctor Gideon Mantell and his wife Mary. Other scientists of the day thought they were the teeth of fish, or of a hippopotamus. But Mantell realized the teeth were from a plant-eating reptile like a modern iguana lizard. His first reconstructions showed a kind of a dragon-sized, iguana-like reptile, similar to the first reconstructions of the meat-eating *Megalosaurus*, also recently discovered.

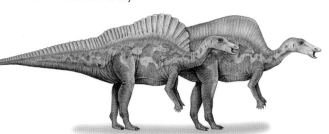

MUTTABURRASAURUS

TENONTOSAURUS

CHANGING FACE

Over the years, as more specimens were found, *Iguanodon's* appearance changed. In the 1850s, it was constructed in the Crystal Palace gardens in London, along the lines of Mantell's big lizard. Then, in 1878, a whole herd of *Iguanodon* skeletons, mostly complete, were found in a coal mine in Bernissart, Belgium. These animals were up to 33 feet (10 m) long and had hind legs that were much longer than their forelimbs. This evidence led to reconstructions of *Iguanodon* sitting on its hind legs, resting on its tail like a kangaroo—an image that was accepted for the next century.

TRIASSIC 248-206 MYA	EARLY/MID JURASSIC 206-159 MYA	LATE JURASSIC 159-144 MYA	EARLY CRETACEOUS 144-97 MYA	LATE CRETACEOUS 97-65 MYA

THE DUCKBILLS

In the Late Cretaceous, a new group of ornithopods evolved from the iguanodontids. The vegetation was changing: primitive forests were giving way to modern-looking woodlands of oak, beech, and other broad-leaved trees with undergrowth of flowering herbs. These new dinosaurs, the hadrosaurs, spread and flourished in the forests throughout Europe, Asia, and North America. They had thousands of grinding teeth and a broad beak at the front of the mouth.

MODERN CONIFERS

Modern conifers, such as pine and spruce, as well as the broad-leaved trees, such as oak and ash, appeared in Cretaceous times. Until then, the more primitive conifers, such as monkey puzzle trees, had sustained the sauropods. Hadrosaurs were well equipped for dealing with the new conifers. They used their broad beaks to scrape off the needles and their batteries of teeth to grind them down before swallowing.

HADROSAURUS

Hadrosaurus was, like *Iguanodon*, essentially a two-footed, plant-eating dinosaur which as an adult would have been rather too heavy to spend much time on its hind legs. It would have moved about on all fours, a theory confirmed by the fleshy, weight-bearing pads on its forelimbs. *Hadrosaurus'* tail was very deep and flat, which once led scientists to think the hadrosaur may have been a swimming animal—an idea that has now been discarded. Its most distinctive feature was its broad, flat, duck-like beak.

HEAD CRESTS

Some hadrosaurs, like this *Parasaurolophus*, had elaborate head crests. Mostly made of hollow bone connected to the nostrils, they were probably used for signaling one another through dense forests. Each type of hadrosaur had a unique crest shape to distinguish different herds from one another. Those with flat heads or solid crests probably supported an inflatable flap of skin that could have been puffed up like a frog's throat to make a noise.

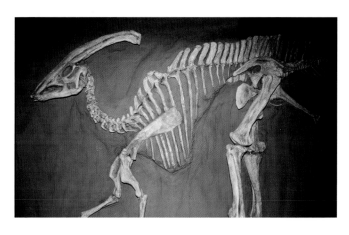

HADROSAURS

SAUROPODS

SPREAD OF DUCKBILLS

The hadrosaurs spread from Europe and became the most important plant-eating dinosaurs in the northern hemisphere. At the time, Europe, Asia, and North America were joined in a single landmass and animals could spread freely. However, South America was an island continent separated from North America by a wide seaway. Hadrosaurs did reach South America but never gained a secure foothold. Long-necked sauropods remained the most important plant eaters in South America until the end of the age of dinosaurs.

TRIASSIC 248-206 MYA	EARLY/MID JURASSIC 206-159 MYA	LATE JURASSIC 159-144 MYA	EARLY CRETACEOUS 144-97 MYA	LATE CRETACEOUS 97-65 MYA

THE PLATED LIZARDS

Not long after ornithopods came into existence, all kinds of other dinosaurs began to evolve from them. Many sported armor of one kind or another. They were too heavy to spend much time on two legs and became mostly four-footed beasts. One group had armor arranged in a double row of plates or spikes down its back and tail. These plated dinosaurs were known as stegosaurids.

PLATE PUZZLES

The back plates of *Stegosaurus* were embedded in its skin but not attached directly to its skeleton. This has caused uncertainty about how they were arranged. One theory suggests that the plates lay flat as armor along the animal's back. Another is that they stood upright in pairs. Yet another says they had a single upright row of overlapping plates. The most widely accepted view is that they stood in a double row, alternating with one another. Some scientists suggest that the muscles at the base of the plates would have allowed *Stegosaurus* to point them at an attacker.

FLAT   PAIRS

SINGLE OVERLAPPING ROW   DOUBLE ALTERNATING

UNDER ATTACK

STEGOSAURUS

Stegosaurus lived in North America at the end of the Jurassic Period. A big four-footed animal up to 26 feet (8 m) long, with shorter legs at the front, a double row of plates along its back, and two pairs of spikes sticking out toward the tip of its tail, it had a small head and a kind of armored mesh protecting its throat. Some scientists believe the plates formed an armored shield. Others insist they acted as heat exchangers to cool its blood by turning the plates to the wind or to absorb warmth from the Sun.

DEATH OF DENVER STEGOSAURUS

A team from the Denver Museum discovered a *Stegosaurus* skeleton with a diseased tail after a broken tail spike became infected. The weakened animal then died during a drought. Its stomach bloated, rolling it over on its back. The drought ended and a nearby river burst its banks, covering the *Stegosaurus* with silt. All this was deduced 140 million years later from the fossil and the types of rocks found nearby. Such study of what leads to fossilization is known as *taphonomy*.

SMALL BRAIN

The head of a *Stegosaurus* was quite small and held a very small brain. Like ornithopods, it had a beak at the front of its mouth and cheeks along the side.

TRIASSIC 248-206 MYA	EARLY/MID JURASSIC 206-159 MYA	LATE JURASSIC 159-144 MYA	EARLY CRETACEOUS 144-97 MYA	LATE CRETACEOUS 97-65 MYA

A WORLD OF STEGOSAURIDS

Stegosaurus was not the only stegosaurid. There were many others, ranging from North America through Europe to Asia. They probably evolved from an Early Jurassic group called the Scelidosaurids. The most primitive of the stegosaurids we know were found in Middle Jurassic rocks in China. From such medium-sized animals developed a wide range of plated and spiked dinosaurs. By the Middle Cretaceous they had all but died out. The remains of an animal that was thought to be a stegosaurid was found in Late Cretaceous rocks in India. It was throught the group lasted longer in India, an island continent at the time. In fact the bones were from a plesiosaur—a sea reptile unrelated to any dinosaur.

CLEVER TAIL

Most stegosaurids had two pairs of spikes at the end of their tail. The tails were usually quite flexible and could have been swung sideways with some force against the flanks of an attacker. In the hipbones was a gap that may have held a concentration of nerves to control the hind legs and tail and a gland that supplied extra energy. This space in the tail gave rise to a once-popular misconception that stegosaurids had two brains.

VARIETY OF STEGOSAURIDS

The most primitive stegosaurid known is the 13-foot- (4-m-) long *Huayangosaurus* from Middle Jurassic China. Later stegosaurids had shorter front legs, but the legs of *Huayangosaurus* hardly varied. Its armor included paired narrow back spikes and a tail with two pairs of spikes. It also had a pair of shoulder spikes, as did some later stegosaurids. *Dacenturus* (Late Jurassic Europe) had low, rounded plates on its shoulders and back and tall spikes down its tail. *Kentrosaurus* (Late Jurassic Africa) had its center of gravity at its hips, so, like some sauropods, it could rise on its hind legs to browse (as could *Stegosaurus*). *Wuerhosaurus* (Early Cretaceous China) was as big as *Stegosaurus* and had long low back plates.

WUERHOSAURUS

DACENTURUS

HUAYANGOSAURUS

EAST AFRICAN DISCOVERIES

The Humboldt Museum in Berlin has a collection of Late Jurassic dinosaurs excavated from East Africa in the 1920s. Among them are the stegosaurid *Kentrosaurus*, which was very similar to the North American *Stegosaurus*. There were also sauropods such as *Dicraeosaurus* (shown left), which was similar to *Diplodocus*.

AN EARLY STEGOSAURID

Cow-sized *Scelidosaurus*, known from the Lower Jurassic rocks of England, was a four-footed herbivore covered with small studs of armor. It may have been an ancestor of the stegosaurids or of the later Cretaceous nodosaurids of North America and the Middle Jurassic to Late Cretaceous ankylosaurids of Europe, North America, and Asia. It may even have been ancestral to both.

KENTROSAURUS

TRIASSIC 248-206 MYA	EARLY/MID JURASSIC 206-159 MYA	LATE JURASSIC 159-144 MYA	EARLY CRETACEOUS 144-97 MYA	LATE CRETACEOUS 97-65 MYA

THE NODOSAURIDS
SPIKY DINOSAURS

As the Jurassic Period passed, the armored stegosaurids became extinct and other groups of armored dinosaurs evolved. The two most closely related groups were the nodosaurids and the ankylosaurids. Each had small, bony plates across their broad backs. These plates stretched up the neck to the head and down the tail and would have had horny covers that made the animal's back impregnable. The distinctive feature of the nodosaurid group was the presence of long, tough spikes sticking out sideways and upward from the shoulders and from the sides.

GASTONIA

One of the best-preserved nodosaurid fossils ever found was *Gastonia*. Its armor formed a solid shield. Spikes stood up over the shoulders, and it had a series of broad, flat spines, almost blades, sticking outward and running down each side from the neck to the tip of the tail. It was found in Early Cretaceous rocks in Utah, but an almost identical Early Cretaceous dinosaur has been found in England.

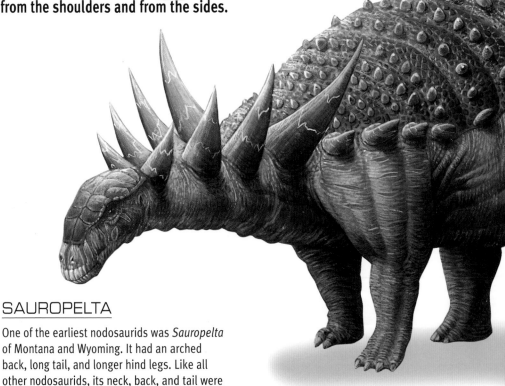

SAUROPELTA

One of the earliest nodosaurids was *Sauropelta* of Montana and Wyoming. It had an arched back, long tail, and longer hind legs. Like all other nodosaurids, its neck, back, and tail were covered with armor. *Sauropelta's* long, defensive spines were confined to the neck and shoulders and spread outward and upward.

SAUROPELTA SKELETON

The solid back plate armor is the most commonly fossilized part of a nodosaurid and is usually found upside down. If a nodosaurid died and fell into a river, it may have been washed out to sea. As it decayed, expanding digestive gases in its gut would have turned it over, its heavy back acting as a keel. As it settled on the seabed, it would be buried and eventually fossilized in that position.

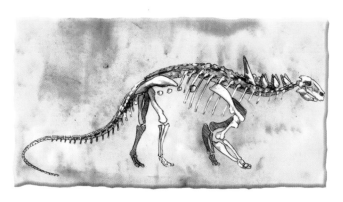

STRUTHIOSAURUS

Not all nodosaurids were big animals. *Struthiosaurus* from Upper Cretaceous rocks of central Europe was only 6.5 feet (2 m) long, with a body the size of a dog. It was probably an island dweller. Island animals, such as the modern Shetland pony, tend to evolve into smaller forms to make best use of limited food.

SPIKY CUSTOMERS

Two related groups of armored dinosaurs existed in Cretaceous times. The nodosaurids were characterized by spikes on the neck and sides, while the ankylosaurids had clubs on the ends of their tails.

TRIASSIC 248-206 MYA	EARLY/MID JURASSIC 206-159 MYA	LATE JURASSIC 159-144 MYA	EARLY CRETACEOUS 144-97 MYA	LATE CRETACEOUS 97-65 MYA

27

ANKYLOSAURIDS
THE CLUB-TAILS

Ankylosaurids were closely related to nodosaurids but mostly came later, toward the end of the Cretaceous. With their armored necks and backs, they looked like their relatives, but instead of having spikes on the shoulders and sides, they had a heavy, bony club at the end of the tail. This could have been devastating when swung at an enemy. It may also have been used as a decoy. Perhaps it looked like a head on a neck, causing meat eaters to attack it instead of the more vulnerable front end.

CRETACEOUS UNDERGROWTH

By the end of the Cretaceous Period, modern plants had evolved. Beneath the broad-leaved trees was an undergrowth of flowering herbs such as buttercups. The ankylosaurids and the nodosaurids carried their heads low and their mouths close to the ground. They were evidently low-level feeders that ate the flowering herbs.

A HEARTY APPETITE

Without its shield of armor, *Euoplocephalus* was a heavy, four-footed animal. Its hips were broad, but the design allowed the intestines to be carried well back. The intestines would have been massive and probably contained fermenting chambers like those of modern cows.

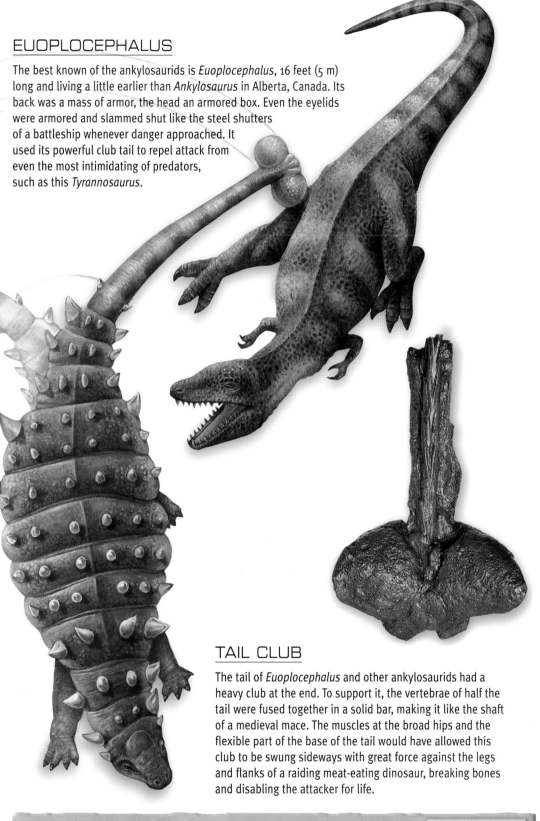

EUOPLOCEPHALUS

The best known of the ankylosaurids is *Euoplocephalus*, 16 feet (5 m) long and living a little earlier than *Ankylosaurus* in Alberta, Canada. Its back was a mass of armor, the head an armored box. Even the eyelids were armored and slammed shut like the steel shutters of a battleship whenever danger approached. It used its powerful club tail to repel attack from even the most intimidating of predators, such as this *Tyrannosaurus*.

TAIL CLUB

The tail of *Euoplocephalus* and other ankylosaurids had a heavy club at the end. To support it, the vertebrae of half the tail were fused together in a solid bar, making it like the shaft of a medieval mace. The muscles at the broad hips and the flexible part of the base of the tail would have allowed this club to be swung sideways with great force against the legs and flanks of a raiding meat-eating dinosaur, breaking bones and disabling the attacker for life.

TRIASSIC 248-206 MYA	EARLY/MID JURASSIC 206-159 MYA	LATE JURASSIC 159-144 MYA	EARLY CRETACEOUS 144-97 MYA	LATE CRETACEOUS 97-65 MYA

BONEHEADS

Imagine a dinosaur, a two-footed, plant-eating dinosaur such as an ornithopod, but give it a very high forehead so it looks brainy. What you would have is a pachycephalosaurid—another dinosaur group descended from the ornithopods. The intelligent look is actually false. The brain in that head is tiny, and the roof of the skull is made up of thick bone. We think the bone on top of the head was a weapon—a kind of battering ram. This was probably not for use against predators but for display in courtship battles.

ALL CREATURES GREAT AND SMALL

There was a great range of sizes in pachycephalosaurids. The largest known, at 16 feet (5 m) long, was North American *Pachycephalosaurus*. The smallest was *Micropachycephalosaurus* from China, which was about the size of a rabbit. This very small dinosaur has the longest dinosaur name ever given.

HORNED BATTLERS

Stegoceras is the most complete known pachycephalosaurid. Its head bone and strong neck provided great protection. They seem to have lived in herds. The males probably fought each other to lead the herd; the strongest would mate with the females.

HARD HEADS

Dinosaur skulls are rarely preserved as fossils, but pachycephalosaurid skulls were different. The top bone of the skull was so massive it often survived as a fossil. Commonly the only part of the animal preserved, these skulls are often found very battered. This suggests they were washed down a river for long distances before being buried in sediment. This may mean that these were mountain-living animals.

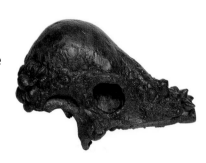

HEADS

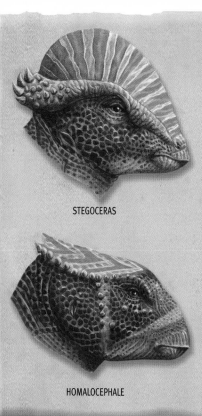

STEGOCERAS

STYGIMOLOCH

Each group of pachycephalosaurids had its own type of skull shape and ornamentation. *Stegoceras* and *Homalocephale*, from Mongolia, had sloping heads, higher at the rear, the latter with an elaborate head crest. *Prenocephale*, also from Mongolia, had a more rounded, dome-like head. Both had decorative lumps around the bony crown. North American *Stygimoloch* was perhaps the strangest, with a weird array of spikes and spines all around its dome. These were probably used for intimidation rather than fighting. All pachycephalosaurids lived in the Late Cretaceous Period.

HOMALOCEPHALE

PRENOCEPHALE

MODERN SPARRERS

In the North American Rocky Mountains, modern bighorn sheep and mountain goats go through an annual ritual in which the males fight the flock leader to test his strength. The construction of their skulls and horns protects them from suffering much damage when they bash against one another. Pachycephalosaurids probably had similar rituals.

TRIASSIC 248-206 MYA	EARLY/MID JURASSIC 206-159 MYA	LATE JURASSIC 159-144 MYA	EARLY CRETACEOUS 144-97 MYA	LATE CRETACEOUS 97-65 MYA

THE PRIMITIVE
HORNED DINOSAURS

The last of the plant-eating dinosaur groups existed from the mid- to Late Cretaceous. Like the ankylosaurids and the nodosaurids, they lived in North America and in Asia, and they also evolved from ornithopods. They were equipped with armor, but it was confined solely to the head. Early types were lightly built and very ornithopod-like, but in later forms the armor on the head became so heavy that they moved around as four-footed animals. Flamboyant neck shields and horns evolved, and these horned dinosaurs became known as the ceratopsians.

ARCHAEOCERATOPS

The most primitive of the ceratopsians known is *Archaeoceratops*. It was a very small animal, about 3 feet (1 m) long, and scampered nimbly on hind legs on the plains of Early Cretaceous China. It had a head that was very similar to that of *Psittacosaurus*. Its skeleton was so primitive and generalized it is possible that its descendants gave rise to the big ceratopsians that were to follow.

CYCAD FOSSIL

At the end of the Cretaceous Period, the old-style vegetation was largely replaced by modern species of plants. However, some of the older types of palmlike cycads remained in some regions. In the areas where they occurred, the ceratopsians may have relied on these plants. Their narrow beaks could have reached into the palmlike clump of fronds and selected the best pieces, and their strong jaws could have shredded the tough leaves.

TRIASSIC 248-206 MYA	EARLY/MID JURASSIC 206-159 MYA	LATE JURASSIC 159-144 MYA	EARLY CRETACEOUS 144-97 MYA	LATE CRETACEOUS 97-65 MYA

AN EARLY SHEEP

Scientists regard *Protoceratops* as the sheep of Late Cretaceous Mongolia. Similar in size to sheep, they lived in herds and grazed the sparse vegetation of the arid landscape. One particular skeleton was found with the skeleton of a fierce carnivore, *Velociraptor*, clinging to its head shield. The meat eater had attacked the ceratopsian with its killing claws, but the ceratopsian must have fought back with its big beak; both dinosaurs lost their lives during the fight.

WHO'S A PRETTY BOY?

An early relative of the ceratopsians was the 5-foot- (1.5-m-) long parrot-lizard *Psittacosaurus*. It developed a very strong beak and powerful jaws for plucking and chopping the tough vegetation it ate. A bony ridge around the back of the skull anchored its strong jaw muscles. The bony ridge and its big beak gave the skull a square shape, and the head must have looked a bit like the big-beaked head of a modern parrot.

BIG BROTHER

By the time *Montanoceratops* had evolved, toward the end of the Late Cretaceous, ceratopsians were bigger and had developed horns. *Montanoceratops* was about 10 feet (3 m) long and walked on all fours. Like its two-footed ancestors, however, it had claws on its feet. In later ceratopsians, the toenails developed into hooves, which were better able to carry the weight of big animals.

THE BIG-HORNED DINOSAURS

WILDEBEEST

The big ceratopsians were probably the most spectacular Late Cretaceous dinosaurs. They were all four-footed and mostly as big as today's rhinoceros. The ridge of bone around the neck had evolved into a broad shield. They also had an array of long horns on the face. The skulls of the big ceratopsians were so tough that many were preserved as fossils. There were two main lines of evolution. One group developed long frills and a pair of long horns above the eyes; the other had shorter frills and tended to have a single horn on the nose.

We know ceratopsians moved in herds because we have found bone beds consisting of many hundreds, even thousands, of skeletons. The animals would have been migrating, traveling in herds to areas where there was more food at a particular time of year. When crossing a river, they may have been caught by a sudden flash flood that washed them away and dumped their bodies. This still happens in Africa today as herds of wildebeest migrate from one feeding ground to another.

TRICERATOPS

The biggest and most famous of the ceratopsians is *Triceratops*. Although it belonged to the short-frilled lineage that tended to have horns only on the nose, *Triceratops* also had long horns above its eyes. It grew to about 29 feet (9 m) long and weighed up to 6 tons. Several species of *Triceratops* roamed the plains between Alberta, Canada, and Colorado at the end of the Cretaceous Period. Like all ceratopsians, it had a shield, which was probably used to protect its neck and shoulders, but it may also have been used for display or for heat regulation (*see pages 22–23*).

ALL FOR ONE

The horns of ceratopsians would have been used to defend themselves and their herd against big carnivores and also to tussle with one another over position in the herd. Having locked horns, they would have pushed and shoved until one of them gave way. Little harm would have come to the loser. While traveling, the ceratopsians may have kept their young at the center of the herd to protect them. If attacked by carnivores they may have formed a circle with the youngsters in the center and the adults facing outward so that the attackers were faced with the shields and horns of all the herd. Today, musk-oxen protect their herd in this way.

VARIETY OF HEADS

Ceratopsians all had the same body shape, but their different shapes of shield and horn arrangements made each type easily recognizable to its own herd. *Styracosaurus* had a monumental horn on its nose and an array of horns around its shield. *Chasmosaurus* had an enormous, sail-like shield. *Einiosaurus* had a long nose horn that curved forward and a pair of straight horns at the edge of its shield. *Acheluosaurus* had a battering ram on its nose, a pair of short, bladelike horns above its eyes, and a curved pair at the shield-edge.

EINIOSAURUS

ACHELUOSAURUS

CHASMOSAURUS

STYRACOSAURUS

TRIASSIC 248-206 MYA	EARLY/MID JURASSIC 206-159 MYA	LATE JURASSIC 159-144 MYA	EARLY CRETACEOUS 144-97 MYA	LATE CRETACEOUS 97-65 MYA

DID YOU KNOW?

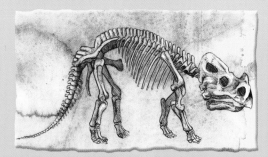

Most dinosaur skulls were made of lightweight struts of bone, loosely articulated. After death they usually fell to bits and were lost. That is why we have so few dinosaur skulls. For example we know of about 120 species of long-necked sauropod, but we have skulls for only eight of them.

We did not have the skull of the most famous sauropod *Apatosaurus* (*see page 13*) for a long time. For about a century we thought that it had a tall boxy skull like *Brachiosaurus*. When the skull was finally found it was long and narrow like that of *Diplodocus*.

The only dinosaur skulls that are quite common are those of the boneheads (*see pages 30–31*) and the ceratopsians (*see pages 34–35*). Both groups had armored heads made up of massive pieces of fused bone.

The skull of the small ceratopsian *Protoceratops* (*see page 33*) is often found in the bleak deserts of Mongolia. Because it is big and has a beak like that of an eagle, it may be that these discoveries led to the myth of the gryphon—a fabulous animal that was part eagle and part lion.

The deepest dinosaur fossil comes from the North Sea, between Scotland and Norway. A prosauropod (*see pages 6–9*) was found by oil drillers at a depth of 1.4 miles (2.3 km) beneath the bed of the sea.

There were two types of duckbill (*see pages 20–21*). One type had a very broad beak while the other had a beak that was quite narrow. The broad-beaked type would have taken great mouthfuls of food, eating all sorts of things indiscriminately, while the narrow-beaked type would have been more choosy, selecting particular plants to eat.

We see a similar difference between the mouths of the two types of armoured dinosaur. The nodosaurids (*see pages 26–27*) had a narrow mouth, suggesting feeding on particular plants, while the ankylosaurids (*see pages 28–29*) had a broad mouth and took great mouthfuls of anything that grew close to the ground.

The titanosaurids (*see page 14*) had no toes on their front feet. They walked on stumpy hand bones.

The sauropods went on migrations, probably moving to new feeding sites as the seasons changed. We know this because of the masses of footprints we have found, showing great herds of these animals all going in the same direction. In South America there are sauropod nesting sites. It seems that the animals returned to the same place every year to lay their eggs.

The most famous skeleton of *Diplodocus* (*see pages 10–11*) was that excavated in 1902 by a team from the Carnegie Museum in Pittsburgh,

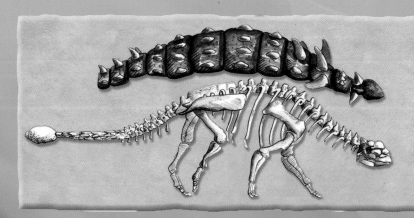

with the financial backing of the steel magnate
Andrew Carnegie. The philanthropist was so
impressed that he had plaster casts made of all
300 bones so that 10 replica skeletons could be
sent to other museums around the world. The
contractor for this job was Serafini Augustini, who
made religious medallions and plaster saints in a
shop close to the museum.

**Palaeopathology is the study of ancient diseases,
and can be applied to the skeletons of dinosaurs.**
Several skulls of *Triceratops* (*see pages 34–35*)
have suffered damage, showing holes that match
the shape of a *Triceratops* horn. This is interpreted
as the result of two individuals fighting one
another. *Iguanodon* (*see pages 18–19*) foot bones
are sometimes fused together through arthritis—
damage probably due to excessive weight. In the
Denver Natural History Museum there is a duckbill
(*see pages 20–21*) with a *Tyrannosaurus*-mouth-
shaped bite out of the backbone. This one was
lucky to escape!

**Trace fossils are the remains of an animal's
lifestyle, rather than the remains of the animal
itself.** Trace fossils cover footprints, trackways,
droppings, eggs, and nesting sites. These tell
more about the dinosaur than the remains of the
animal itself. After all, a single dinosaur may leave
millions of footprints throughout its life, but only
one skeleton.

There are several types of dinosaur skeleton. The
most spectacular is the "articulated skeleton." In
this, all the bones are joined together as they were
in life. Then there is the "associated skeleton"
which consists of a jumble of bones that evidently
come from the same animal. The associated
skeleton tends to be more important to science, as
it can be studied more thoroughly—people are
reluctant to disturb something as beautiful as an
articulated skeleton. More commonly the fossil
comes as an isolated bone. Finally, there are
scraps of bone that don't seem to relate to
anything at all, and have no scientific value. These
are termed "float." Some excavations map every
single piece of float in the hope that some day
something will be made of its distribution, but
most excavations do not bother.

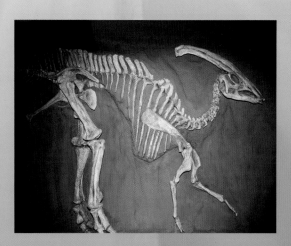

SUMMARY TIMELINE

PLATEOSAURUS

Thecodontosaurus
Euskelosaurus
Melanorosaurus
Plateosaurus
Riojasaurus

TRIASSIC/JURASSIC
BOUNDARY

Huayangosaurus
Shunosaurus

MIDDLE/UPPER
JURASSIC
BOUNDARY

200

161

300

251
BEGINNING OF
TRIASSIC
PERIOD

175
LOWER/
MIDDLE
JURASSIC
BOUNDARY

Anchisaurus
Lufengosaurus
Scelidosaurus
Ammosaurus
Heterodontosaurus

LUFENGOSAURUS

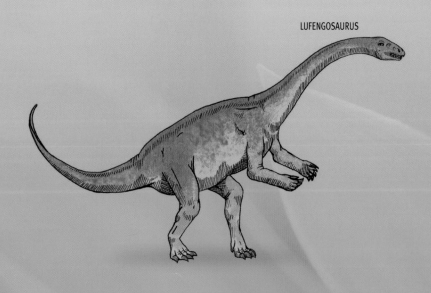

Archaeoceratops
Psittacosaurus
Sauropelta
Mutaburrasaurus
Tenontosaurus
Ouranosaurus
Gastonia
Sauroposeidon
Amargasaurus
Hypsilophodon
Iguanodon
Wuerhosaurus

**LOWER/UPPER
CRETACEOUS
BOUNDARY**

HYPSILOPHODON

99

145   100   65   0

**JURASSIC/
CRETACEOUS
BOUNDARY**

**END OF
CRETACEOUS
PERIOD**

million
years ago

Brachytrachelopan
Stegosaurus
Miragaia
Diplodocus
Apatosaurus
Brachiosaurus
Giraffatitan
Kentrosaurus
Tianyulong

Triceratops
Torosaurus
Chasmosaurus
Styracosaurus
Einiosaurus
Achelousaurus
Montanaceratops
Homalocephale
Pachycephalosaurus
Stygimoloch
Alamosaurus
Euoplocephalus
Saltasaurus
Hadrosaurus
Struthiosaurus
Prenocephale
Stegoceras
Protoceratops
Argentinosaurus
Gasparinasaura
Oryctodromeus

STEGOSAURUS

SALTASAURUS

39

WHERE DID THEY LIVE?

Where there are plants there are plant-eating animals to eat them. The herbivorous dinosaurs fell in with this law and diversified all across the globe, adapting to the different types of vegetation that existed in the different places.

Our knowledge of this is growing all the time. Between 1992 and 2004 there was an increase of 55 percent in the number of dinosaur sites known.

The first plant-eating dinosaurs to evolve—the prosauropods (*see pages 6–9*) and, to a lesser extent, the small ornithopods (*see pages 16–17*)—appeared in the desert landscape with oases of the late Triassic, just as the carnivorous dinosaurs did. We know the fossils of the earliest prosauropods from the Triassic rocks of Arizona and of South Africa. There they browsed the newly evolved coniferous trees and fed from the ferns, tree ferns, and horsetails that had been around for many millions of years up to that point. There are over a hundred Triassic dinosaur sites in the world, 33 of them from North America alone. However only two thirds of these North America localities have yielded the remains of herbivorous dinosaurs. In the United States we know prosauropod remains from Arizona, Texas, and Pennsylvania, and prosauropod footprints from New Mexico. We also have ornithopod remains from Arizona, New Mexico, Texas, and North Carolina, with tracks known from New Jersey, Pennsylvania, and Virginia.

Jurassic dinosaur remains are much more abundant than those of the Triassic. The early Jurassic dinosaur-bearing rocks are found more or less in the same areas as the Triassic, but as the age drew onward and habitable conditions spread over the continent, more and more areas seemed to support dinosaur life. Dinosaur-bearing rocks dating from the end of the period are nearly all found in the Morrison Formation, a vast swathe of mudstones and river sandstones, stretching through Arizona, Colorado, Kansas, Montana, North Dakota, South Dakota, Nebraska, New Mexico, Oklahoma, Utah, Wyoming, a corner of Texas and right up into Canada. From here we find the remains of sauropods (*see pages 10–13*), ornithopods (*see pages 16–17*), stegosaurids

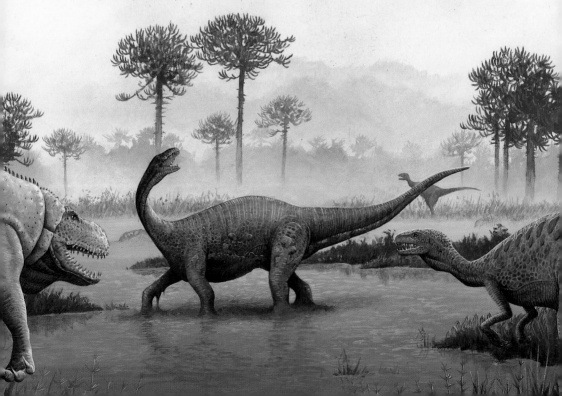

(see pages 22–25), and a few small early armored dinosaurs (see pages 26–29). These browsed the forests of conifers, ginkgoes, and tree ferns, and the undergrowth of ferns and horsetails that clothed the banks of the rivers and the shores of the lakes.

As the subsequent Cretaceous period drew on, the arid center of the continent was covered by a broad shallow sea that spread southward from northern Canada, covering the whole of the area of the Jurassic Morrison formation, and cut the landmass completely in two. Dinosaurs were now confined to the shorelines of this inland sea. Trackways tell us that herds of ornithopods like *Iguanodon* (see pages 18–19) used the beaches of this sea as a highway in their north-south migrations. In the west of this sea the newly-forming Rocky Mountains rose steeply. The plains between the sea and the mountains supported herds of horned dinosaurs such as *Triceratops* (see pages 34–35), in the northern forests dwelled herds of duckbills (see pages 20–21) such as *Hadrosaurus*, while in the foothills of the mountains the coniferous trees were browsed by the last of the sauropods (see pages 11–15) such as *Alamosaurus*.

Across the world it is the same picture. We only get the remains of dinosaurs in rocks that were laid down at the time the dinosaurs were alive, and that have not since been eroded away. In the Triassic and early Jurassic, as we have seen, there are the same plant-eating dinosaurs appearing all over the world. Even in the late Jurassic we find similar sauropods in East Africa as existed in the Morrison Formation of North America—close relatives of *Brachiosaurus* and *Diplodocus*.

Then, in Cretaceous times, the picture began to change. The continents broke up and the pieces began to drift apart. This had a profound effect on which dinosaurs lived where. North America remained joined to Asia, across the Bering Sea, and there was free movement of dinosaur types between the two continents. The remains of duckbills and horned dinosaurs are found on both. Likewise South America, Antarctica, and Australia remained joined for some time. But these continents were a long way from the northern ones. The main plant-eaters on the northern continents were the duckbills, but they never reached the southern continents. There the sauropods, particularly the titanosaurids (see pages 14–15) thrived until the end of the age of dinosaurs.

NEW DISCOVERIES

The stegosaurids (*see pages 22–25*) become stranger and stranger. Newly discovered *Miragaia* from Portugal had a long neck, making it look like one of the long-necked sauropods.

And a new sauropod *Brachytrachelopan* from South America was like *Diplodocus* but had a very short neck—just enough to allow it to reach the ground. This made it look like one of the stegosaurids.

Now we know that some dinosaurs actually burrowed into the ground. *Oryctodromeus*, a small ornithopod (*see pages 16–17*) with strong digging arms, was found in a fossilized burrow in Montana. The burrow had collapsed and buried an adult and some little ones. Now similar burrows are being discovered in Australia.

New fossils of duckbilled dinosaurs have been found in Montana and North Dakota that are so well preserved that we have even found traces of skin and the internal organs. Usually we don't get that—just bones.

Scientists have now been able to reproduce the chemical reactions that took place in a sauropod's stomach. We used to think that their food—consisting of the primitive conifers and tree ferns—was not very nutritious. The new experiments show that there was actually a great deal of energy generated from such a diet once the stomach chemicals got to work.

New work on how dinosaur skulls grow may wipe out many of the dinosaur species that we now know. As the skulls grew, some parts grew faster than others, and some parts withered away. This meant that the skull shapes changed throughout life. The whole range of boneheads (*see pages 30–31*) may represent a single species that changed the size of the dome and the arrangement of the horns and bumps as the individuals grew up. The small spiny ones may be juveniles, while the big ones with heavy domes may be adults. The same with the ceratopsians (*see pages 34–35*). The biggest dinosaur skull known belonged to *Torosaurus*—like *Triceratops*, but with a very long neck shield with holes in it. Now it is possible that *Torosaurus* is just an elderly *Triceratops*, and the frill changed shape as it grew—growing longer and developing the holes.

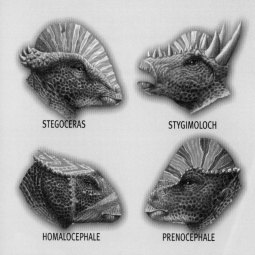

STEGOCERAS   STYGIMOLOCH

HOMALOCEPHALE   PRENOCEPHALE

We used to think that dinosaurs did not eat grass, because grass had not evolved in dinosaur times. Recently, however, remains of grass pollen have been found in the fossilized innards of a sauropod in India. So there was grass around at the time, and some dinosaurs did eat it, but it is unlikely to have been a main source of food for them. Open grasslands did not develop until well into the age of mammals, which was long after the dinosaurs became extinct.

Dinosaurs keep growing—and shrinking! A beautifully preserved duckbill (*see pages 20–21*) has been found in North Dakota. Each vertebra seems to be separated from the next by what would have been a disk of gristle when the animal was alive. This makes the animal as much as 10 per cent longer than was first appreciated. This may well apply to the other dinosaurs.

There have been many exciting discoveries of feathered dinosaurs in the last few years, but we have thought that only the meat-eating dinosaurs had the plumage. Now we know of a plant-eater, *Tianyulong*, that had a covering of primitive feathers. It was a small ornithopod from China (*see pages 16–17*).

On the other hand, it has been found that the mathematics used to calculate the weight of living dinosaurs may have been wrong, and for a long time we have thought that they were much heavier than they really were. Scientists have now put together new equations to estimate dinosaur weight, based on the size of the leg bones and the amount of weight they could carry. The new numbers show that some dinosaurs were about half as heavy as we once thought—for example the sauropod *Apatosaurus* (*see page 13*) did not weigh 38 tons after all—more like 18 tons.

MOVIES, WEBSITES, & FURTHER READING

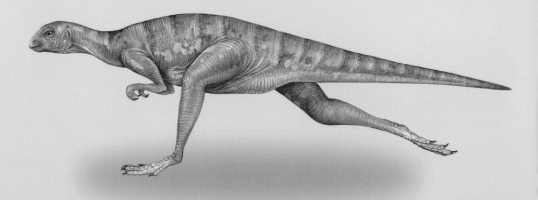

MOVIES

Don't watch movies to get facts about dinosaurs! However, it is interesting to watch dinosaur movies to see how the view of dinosaurs has changed over the years. Here are some examples.

KING KONG (1933)

There was a sauropod in this movie, and it showed many of the features of sauropods that were accepted back at the time, but are now known to be wrong. For one thing, paleontologists thought that sauropods such as *Apatosaurus*, spent much of their time in the water. They thought that they would not have been able to support their own weight on land. *King Kong* features a sauropod doing just this. Also, once it was on land it dragged its tail along the ground. We now know that sauropods held their tails clear of the ground, supported by strong tendons along the backbone. And it is shown eating a man—something no sauropod would ever have done!

The first dinosaur that the explorers see when they explore the island is a *Stegosaurus*. It was far too big and the tail was much too flexible, but that was done for dramatic and artistic reasons. However, the tail had four pairs of spikes on the end, and this was what was believed at the time. We thought that there was a species of *Stegosaurus* that did have four pairs of spikes (instead of two pairs) but we now know that this was based on a skeleton made up from the bones of two individuals.

THE ANIMAL WORLD (1956)

A wildlife documentary that featured a ten minute sequence from the age of dinosaurs.

ONE MILLION YEARS B.C. (1966)

A fantasy that pitted cavemen against dinosaurs, but the dinosaurs were quite nicely sculpted.

JURASSIC PARK (1993)

The most accurate depiction of movie dinosaurs up to that time, but the movie makers took the science and changed it to make it a more exciting story.

This movie also had sauropods wading in the water. That is not to say that they never did so—they just never did so habitually. Incidentally, the book *Jurassic Park* written by Michael Crichton in 1990, is full of scientific errors which the makers of the film wisely avoided. It describes a *Triceratops* eating messily, obviously without the cheek pouches that we now know it to have had. Also it describes *Hypsilophodon* as a climbing, tree-living dinosaur. We used to think so, but not since the 1960s!

In general, in works of fiction, where living dinosaurs are found in a remote area of the world, the area is far too small. Animals as huge as sauropods or big ornithopods would have needed vast feeding areas to support them. Small islands, restricted valleys, and isolated plateaux just would not have the area to support enough food. That is why we find the fossils of dwarf forms in areas that had been islands at that time. It has been estimated that dwarf species of dinosaurs lived on islands less than 50,700 square miles (130,000 square kilometres) in area—about the size of the states of Louisiana or Mississippi. This suggests that full-sized types could not exist on islands smaller than this.

WEBSITES

Wikipedia tends to be distrusted by many people because it is too easy to put spurious information on it. However, the dinosaur material published there is generally quite reliable and up to date.

www.dinosaursociety.com

All sorts of information on dinosaurs, including a valuable frequently updated page giving links to all the dinosaur-related news stories.

www.sciencedaily.com/news/ fossils_ruins/dinosaurs/

A catalog of the dinosaur stories run by this news site.

Warning! *The articles presented by these sites are usually written by journalists, not by dinosaur specialists. As a result they tend to be over-sensational or sometimes plain wrong. If you find an interesting dinosaur news story, it is a good idea to chase it up through different sources, to see how the story differs. Usually, you can tell how much is fact and how much has been made up by the reporter. That's fun, too!*

Google Earth

Key in *DINOSAUR NATIONAL MONUMENT QUARRY VISITOR CENTER*. This will take you to the site of one of the best public exposures of dinosaur remains. You can see little on the Google Earth image, except for the roof of the center, but if you pull back you can see the ridges of exposed rock running east-west (the "strike" in geological parlance), in which the dinosaur remains are found.

Key in *HELL CREEK STATE PARK* and see the kind of badlands landscape in which *Tyrannosaurus* is found.

Key in *CLEVELAND LLOYD DINOSAUR QUARRY*. The circular structure is the parking lot. Just to the north of it are two sheds. These cover the densest collection of Jurassic dinosaur fossils ever found. The remains of over 40 *Allosaurus* have been found there, probably trapped in a swamp while trying to eat plant-eating dinosaurs already trapped there (what we call a "predator trap").

FURTHER READING

THE DINOSAURIA
Edited by David B. Weishampel, Peter Dodson, and Halszka Osmólska, 2nd edition 2004
This is the bible for paleontologists. However, it is extremely technical and hardly to be recommended for the casual reader. And, since the science is constantly changing, the 2nd edition may well be out of date already.

PREHISTORIC TIMES
A quarterly magazine, running since 1993, features articles on dinosaur research and dinosaur lore.
See their website *www.prehistorictimes.com*

GLOSSARY

Ankylosaurid One of a group of armored dinosaurs, that had a club on the tail.

Articulation The way one bone moves as it joins to another.

Carnivore An animal that eats meat.

Ceratopsian One of a group of dinosaurs with armor and horns on the head.

Conifer A tree, like a pine tree, that bears its seeds in a cone.

Cretaceous The period of geological time from 144 to 65 million years ago. The last of the three dinosaur periods.

Cycad A plant that looks rather like a palm tree, but is more closely related to the conifers.

Digestive system The collection of organs in the body that processes food —the stomach, and intestines.

Dinosaur One of a group of reptiles that existed from the Triassic to the Cretaceous periods of Earth's history.

Environment The total of all the surroundings in which an animal or a plant lives—the climate, the vegetation, the terrain, and so on.

Evolve To change from one type of animal to another over generations, in response to changing conditions.

Gastrolith A stone held in the digestive system of some birds and dinosaurs, to help to grind up food.

Hadrosaurid One of a group of ornithopod dinosaurs, which had a duck-like beak.

Heat exchanger A device for extracting heat from round about, or for getting rid of waste heat into the surroundings.

Herb Any plant that grows close to the ground.

Herbivore An animal that eats plants.

Iguana A kind of a plant-eating lizard that lives in the Americas.

Iguanodontid One of a group of ornithopod dinosaurs from which the hadrosaurids evolved.

Jurassic The period of geological time between 206 and 144 million years ago. The heyday of the dinosaurs.

Mammal A warm-blooded animal, usually covered in fur, that gives birth to live offspring and suckles its young.

Migration The movement of animals from one area to another, usually to new feeding grounds.

Morrison Formation A sequence of Upper Jurassic rocks formed from the sediments of rivers and lakes, that spreads from New Mexico to Canada.

Nodosaurid One of a group of armored dinosaurs, that had spikes on the neck and shoulders.

Ornithopod One of a group of dinosaurs with foot bones arranged like those of a bird.

Pachycephalosaurid One of a group of dinosaurs with a dome of thick bone on top of the head.

Paleontologist A scientist who studies paleontology.

Paleontology (Spelled "palaeontology" in Europe). The study of the life of the past.

Prey Animals that are hunted and eaten by other animals.

Prosauropod One of a group of early long-necked plant-eating dinosaurs.

Proto-mammal Once called a "mammal-like reptile," one of a group of animals that shows an evolutionary transition between reptiles and mammals.

Pubic bone One of the bones of the hip.

Reptile A cold-blooded animal that reproduces by laying eggs, and is usually covered by a scaly skin. Lizards and snakes are typical modern reptiles.

Rhynchosaur An early plant-eating reptile that preceded the dinosaurs.

Sauropod One of the group of long-necked plant-eating dinosaurs with long necks and tails.

Skull The bony framework of the head and face that protects the brain.

Stegosaurid One of a group of dinosaurs with plates down the back.

Titanosaurid One of a group of later sauropods.

Triassic The period of geological time between 248 and 206 million years ago, that saw the beginning of the age of the dinosaurs.

Vertebrae The bones of the neck, back, and tail.

INDEX

ACKNOWLEDGMENTS

The publishers would like to thank Advocate, Helen Wire,
and Elizabeth Wiggans for their assistance.

Picture Credits: t=top, b=bottom, c=center, l=left, r=right
Lisa Alderson: 15br, 18b, 19b, 20b, 28–29c, 32–33c. John Alston: 8tl, 8tr, 8b, 13cr, 14t, 22b, 24t, 25c,
31t, 35t, 36t. Australian Museum: 13tl. A–Z Botanical: 21bl, 23tr, 31cr. BBC Natural History Unit: 32b,
36b. Dr. Jose Bonaparte: 9t. Fossil Finds: 11t, 17t, 34cl, 35b. Humboldt Museum: 13cl. National Trust:
13cl. Simon Mendez: 8–9c, 10t, 10–11c, 12–13c, 14–15b, 16b, 20–21c, 24–25c, 26–27c, 30–31c, 32t,
36–37c. Museum of Utah: 31t. Natural History Museum: 18t, 18cl, 18–19b, 20ct, 23t, 24b, 27cr, 28cl,
28b, 30b, 31cr, 33b, 33tr, 35br. Luis Rey: 16t, 17c, 22–23c, 34–35c, 32cl. Professor Kent Stephens: 12t.

NOTE TO READERS
The website addresses are correct at the time of publishing. However, due to the ever-changing
nature of the Internet, websites and content may change. Some websites can contain links that
are unsuitable for children. The publisher is not responsible for changes in content or website
addresses. We advise that Internet searches should be supervised by an adult.